Robert Louis Stevenson, An Elegy & Other Poems by Richard Le Gaillienne

TO MY DEAR MOTHER AND FATHER THESE POEMS ARE LOVINGLY DEDICATED

Richard Thomas Gallienne was born in Liverpool on 20th January, 1866.

His first job was in an accountant's office, but this was quickly abandoned to pursue his first love as a professional writer. His first work, My Ladies' Sonnets, was published in 1887.

In 1889 he became, for a brief time, literary secretary to Wilson Barrett the manager, actor, and playwright. Barrett enjoyed immense success with the staging of melodramas, which would later reach a peak with the historical tragedy The Sign of the Cross (1895).

Le Gallienne joined the staff of The Star newspaper in 1891, and also wrote for various other papers under the pseudonym 'Logroller'. He contributed to the short-lived but influential quarterly periodical The Yellow Book, published between 1894 and 1897.

His first wife, Mildred Lee, died in 1894 leaving their daughter, Hesper, in his care.

In 1897 he married the Danish journalist Julie Norregard. However, the marriage would not be a success. She left him in 1903 and took their daughter Eva to live in Paris. They were eventually divorced in June 1911.

Le Gallienne now moved to the United States and became resident there.

On 27th October 1911, he married Mrs. Irma Perry, whose marriage to her first cousin, the painter and sculptor Roland Hinton Perry, had been dissolved in 1904. Le Gallienne and Irma had known each other for many years and had written an article together a few years earlier in 1906.

Le Gallienne and Irma lived in Paris from the late 1920s, where Irma's daughter Gwen was by then an established figure in the expatriate bohème. Le Gallienne also added a regular newspaper column to the frequent publication of his poems, essays and other articles.

By 1930 Le Gallienne's book publishing career had virtually ceased. During the latter years of that decade Le Gallienne lived in Menton on the French Riviera and, during the war years, in nearby Monaco. His house was commandeered by German troops and his handsome library was nearly sent back to Germany as bounty. Le Gallienne managed a successful appeal to a German officer in Monaco which allowed him to return to Menton to collect his books.

To his credit Le Gallienne refused to write propaganda for the local German and Italian authorities, and financially was often in dire need. On one occasion he collapsed in the street due to hunger.

Richard Thomas Gallienne died on 15th September 1947. He is buried in Menton in a grave whose lease is, at present, due to expire in 2023.

Index of Contents

ROBERT LOUIS STEVENSON

AN ELEGY

High on his Patmos of the Southern Seas
Our northern dreamer sleeps,
Strange stars above him, and above his grave
Strange leaves and wings their tropic splendours wave,
While, far beneath, mile after shimmering mile,
The great Pacific, with its faery deeps,
Smiles all day long its silken secret smile.

Son of a race nomadic, finding still
Its home in regions furthest from its home,

Ranging untired the borders of the world,
And resting but to roam;
Loved of his land, and making all his boast
The birthright of the blood from which he came,
Heir to those lights that guard the Scottish coast,
And caring only for a filial fame;
Proud, if a poet, he was Scotsman most,
And bore a Scottish name.

Death, that long sought our poet, finds at last,
Death, that pursued him over land and sea:
Not his the flight of fear, the heart aghast
With stony dread of immortality,
He fled 'not cowardly';
Fled, as some captain, in whose shaping hand
Lie the momentous fortunes of his land,
Sheds not vainglorious blood upon the field,
Death! why at last he finds his treasure isle,
And he the pirate of its hidden hoard;
Life! 'twas the ship he sailed to seek it in,
And Death is but the pilot come aboard,
Methinks I see him smile a boy's glad smile
On maddened winds and waters, reefs unknown,
As thunders in the sail the dread typhoon,
And in the surf the shuddering timbers groan;
Horror ahead, and Death beside the wheel:
Then—spreading stillness of the broad lagoon,
And lap of waters round the resting keel.

Strange Isle of Voices! must we ask in vain,
In vain beseech and win no answering word,
Save mocking echoes of our lonely pain
From lonely hill and bird?
Island beneath whose unrelenting coast,
As though it never in the sun had been,
The whole world's treasure lieth sunk and lost,
Unsunned, unseen.
For, either sunk beyond the diver's skill,
There, fathoms deep, our gold is all arust,
Or in that island it is hoarded still.
Yea, some have said, within thy dreadful wall
There is a folk that know not death at all,
The loved we lost, the lost we love, are there.
Will no kind voice make answer to our cry,
Give to our aching hearts some little trust,
Show how 'tis good to live, but best to die?
Some voice that knows
Whither the dead man goes:
We hear his music from the other side,
Maybe a little tapping on the door,
A something called, a something sighed—

No more.
O for some voice to valiantly declare
The best news true!
Then, Happy Island of the Happy Dead,
How gladly would we spread
Impatient sail for you!

O vanished loveliness of flowers and faces,
Treasure of hair, and great immortal eyes,
Are there for these no safe and secret places?
And is it true that beauty never dies?
Soldiers and saints, haughty and lovely names,
Women who set the whole wide world in flames,
Poets who sang their passion to the skies,
And lovers wild and wise:
Fought they and prayed for some poor flitting gleam,
Was all they loved and worshipped but a dream?
Is Love a lie and fame indeed a breath,
And is there no sure thing in life—but death?
Or may it be, within that guarded shore,
He meets Her now whom I shall meet no more
Till kind Death fold me 'neath his shadowy wing:
She whom within my heart I softly tell
That he is dead whom once we loved so well,
He, the immortal master whom I sing.

Immortal! yea, dare we the word again,
If aught remaineth of our mortal day,
That which is written—shall it not remain?
That which is sung, is it not built for aye?
Faces must fade, for all their golden looks,
Unless some poet them eternalise,
Make live those golden looks in golden books;
Death, soon or late, will quench the brightest eyes—
'Tis only what is written never dies.
Yea, memories that guard like sacred gold
Some sainted face, they also must grow old,
Pass and forget, and think—or darest thou not!—
On all the beauty that is quite forgot.

Strange craft of words, strange magic of the pen,
Whereby the dead still talk with living men;
Whereby a sentence, in its trivial scope,
May centre all we love and all we hope;
And in a couplet, like a rosebud furled,
Lie all the wistful wonder of the world.

Old are the stars, and yet they still endure,
Old are the flowers, yet never fail the spring:
Why is the song that is so old so new,
Known and yet strange each sweet small shape and hue?

How may a poet thus for ever sing,
Thus build his climbing music sweet and sure,
As builds in stars and flowers the Eternal mind?
Ah, Poet, that is yours to seek and find!
Yea, yours that magisterial skill whereby
God put all Heaven in a woman's eye,
Nature's own mighty and mysterious art
That knows to pack the whole within the part:
The shell that hums the music of the sea,
The little word big with Eternity,
The cosmic rhythm in microcosmic things—
One song the lark and one the planet sings,
One kind heart beating warm in bird and tree—
To hear it beat, who knew so well as he?

Virgil of prose! far distant is the day
When at the mention of your heartfelt name
Shall shake the head, and men, oblivious, say:
'We know him not, this master, nor his fame.'
Not for so swift forgetfulness you wrought,
Day upon day, with rapt fastidious pen,
Turning, like precious stones, with anxious thought,
This word and that again and yet again,
Seeking to match its meaning with the world;
Nor to the morning stars gave ears attent,
That you, indeed, might ever dare to be
With other praise than immortality
Unworthily content.

Not while a boy still whistles on the earth,
Not while a single human heart beats true,
Not while Love lasts, and Honour, and the Brave,
Has earth a grave,
O well-beloved, for you!

AN ODE TO SPRING

(TO GRANT AND NELLIE ALLEN)

Is it the Spring?
  Or are the birds all wrong
That play on flute and viol,
  A thousand strong,
In minstrel galleries
  Of the long deep wood,
Epiphanies
  Of bloom and bud.

Grave minstrels those,

Of deep responsive chant;
But see how yonder goes,
  Dew-drunk, with giddy slant,
Yon Shelley-lark,
  And hark!
Him on the giddy brink
  Of pearly heaven
His fairy anvil clink.

Or watch, in fancy,
  How the brimming note
Falls, like a string of pearls,
  From out his heavenly throat;
Or like a fountain
  In Hesperides,
Raining its silver rain,
  In gleam and chime,
On backs of ivory girls—
  Twice happy rhyme!

Ah, none of these
  May make it plain,
No image we may seek
  Shall match the magic of his gurgling beak.

And many a silly thing
  That hops and cheeps,
And perks his tiny tail,
  And sideway peeps,
And flitters little wing,
  Seems in his consequential way
To tell of Spring.

The river warbles soft and runs
  With fuller curve and sleeker line,
Though on the winter-blackened hedge
  Twigs of unbudding iron shine,
And trampled still the river sedge.

And O the Sun!
  I have no friend so generous as this Sun
That comes to meet me with his big warm hands.
  And O the Sky!
There is no maid, how true,
  Is half so chaste
As the pure kiss of greening willow wands
  Against the intense pale blue
Of this sweet boundless overarching waste.

And see!—dear Heaven, but it is the Spring!—
  See yonder, yonder, by the river there,

Long glittering pearly fingers flash
  Upon the warm bright air:
Why, 'tis the heavenly palm,
  The Christian tree,
Whose budding is a psalm
  Of natural piety:
Soft silver notches up the smooth green stem—
  Ah, Spring must follow them,
It is the Spring!

O Spirit of Spring,
  Whose strange instinctive art
Makes the bird sing,
  And brings the bud again;
O in my heart
  Take up thy heavenly reign,
And from its deeps
  Draw out the hidden flower,
And where it sleeps,
  Throughout the winter long,
O sweet mysterious power
  Awake the slothful song!

February 7, 1893.

TREE-WORSHIP

(TO JOHN LANE)

Vast and mysterious brother, ere was yet of me
  So much as men may poise upon a needle's end,
Still shook with laughter all this monstrous might of thee,
  And still with haughty crest it called the morning friend.

Thy latticed column jetted up the bright blue air,
  Tall as a mast it was, and stronger than a tower;
Three hundred winters had beheld thee mighty there,
  Before my little life had lived one little hour.

With rocky foot stern-set like iron in the land,
  With leafy rustling crest the morning sows with pearls,
Huge as a minster, half in heaven men saw thee stand,
  Thy rugged girth the waists of fifty Eastern girls.

Knotted and warted, slabbed and armoured like the hide
  Of tropic elephant; unstormable and steep
As some grim fortress with a princess-pearl inside,
  Where savage guardian faces beard the bastioned keep:

So hard a rind, old tree, shielding so soft a heart—
  A woman's heart of tender little nestling leaves;
Nor rind so hard but that a touch so soft can part,
  And Spring's first baby-bud an easy passage cleaves.

I picture thee within with dainty satin sides,
  Where all the long day through the sleeping dryad dreams,
But when the moon bends low and taps thee thrice she glides,
  Knowing the fairy knock, to bask within her beams.

And all the long night through, for him with eyes and ears,
  She sways within thine arms and sings a fairy tune,
Till, startled with the dawn, she softly disappears,
  And sleeps and dreams again until the rising moon.

But with the peep of day great bands of heavenly birds
  Fill all thy branchy chambers with a thousand flutes,
And with the torrid noon stroll up the weary herds,
  To seek thy friendly shade and doze about thy roots—

Till with the setting sun they turn them once more home;
  And, ere the moon dawns, for a brief enchanted space,
Weary with million miles, the sore-spent star-beams come,
  And moths and bats hold witches' sabbath in the place.

And then I picture thee some bloodstained Holyrood,
  Dread haunted palace of the bat and owl, whence steal,
Shrouded all day, lost murdered spirits of the wood,
  And fright young happy nests with homeless hoot and squeal.

Then, maybe, dangling from thy gloomy gallows boughs,
  A human corpse swings, mournful, rattling bones and chains—
His eighteenth century flesh hath fattened nineteenth century cows—
  Ghastly Aeolian harp fingered of winds and rains.

Poor Rizpah comes to reap each newly-fallen bone
  That once thrilled soft, a little limb, within her womb;
And mark yon alchemist, with zodiac-spangled zone,
  Wrenching the mandrake root that fattens in the gloom.

So rounds thy day, from maiden morn to haunted night,
  From larks and sunlit dreams to owl and gibbering ghost;
A catacomb of dark, a maze of living light,
  To the wide sea of air a green and welcome coast.

I seek a god, old tree: accept my worship, thou!
  All other gods have failed me always in my need;
I hang my votive song beneath thy temple bough,
  Unto thy strength I cry—Old monster, be my creed!

Give me to clasp this earth with feeding roots like thine,

To mount yon heaven with such star-aspiring head,
Fill full with sap and buds this shrunken life of mine,
   And from my boughs oh! might such stalwart sons be shed.

With loving cheek pressed close against thy horny breast,
   I hear the roar of sap mounting within thy veins;
Tingling with buds, thy great hands open towards the west,
   To catch the sweetheart winds that bring the sister rains.

O winds that blow from out the fruitful mouth of God,
   O rains that softly fall from His all-loving eyes,
You that bring buds to trees and daisies to the sod—
   O God's best Angel of the Spring, in me arise.

A BALLAD OF LONDON

(TO H. W. MASSINSHAM)

Ah, London! London! our delight,
Great flower that opens but at night,
Great City of the Midnight Sun,
Whose day begins when day is done.

Lamp after lamp against the sky
Opens a sudden beaming eye,
Leaping alight on either hand,
The iron lilies of the Strand.

Like dragonflies, the hansoms hover,
With jewelled eyes, to catch the lover;
The streets are full of lights and loves,
Soft gowns, and flutter of soiled doves.

The human moths about the light
Dash and cling close in dazed delight,
And burn and laugh, the world and wife,
For this is London, this is life!

Upon thy petals butterflies,
But at thy root, some say, there lies
A world of weeping trodden things,
Poor worms that have not eyes or wings.

From out corruption of their woe
Springs this bright flower that charms us so,
Men die and rot deep out of sight
To keep this jungle-flower bright.

Paris and London, World-Flowers twain

Wherewith the World-Tree blooms again,
Since Time hath gathered Babylon,
And withered Rome still withers on.

Sidon and Tyre were such as ye,
How bright they shone upon the Tree!
But Time hath gathered, both are gone,
And no man sails to Babylon.

Ah, London! London! our delight,
For thee, too, the eternal night,
And Circe Paris hath no charm
To stay Time's unrelenting arm.

Time and his moths shall eat up all.
Your chiming towers proud and tall
He shall most utterly abase,
And set a desert in their place.

PARIS DAY BY DAY: A FAMILIAR EPISTLE

(TO MRS. HENRY HARLAND)

Paris, half Angel, half Grisette,
I would that I were with thee yet,
Where the long boulevard at even
Stretches its starry lamps to heaven,
And whispers from a thousand trees
Vague hints of the Hesperides.

Once more, once more, my heart, to sit
With Aline's smile and Harry's wit,
To sit and sip the cloudy green,
With dreamy hints of speech between;

Or, may be, flashing all intent
At call of some stern argument,
When the New Woman fain would be,
Like the Old Male, her husband, free.
The prose-man takes his mighty lyre
And talks like music set on fire!

The while the merry crowd slips by
Glittering and glancing to the eye,
All happy lovers on their way
To make a golden end of day—
Ah! Café truly called La Paix!

Or at the pension I would be

With Transatlantic maidens three,
The same, I vow, who once of old
Guarded with song the trees of gold.

O Lady, lady, Vis-à-Vis,
When shall I cease to think of thee,
On whose fair head the Golden Fleece
Too soon, too soon, returns to Greece—
Oh, why to Athens e'er depart?
Come back, come back, and bring my heart!

And she whose gentle silver grace,
So wise of speech and kind of face,
Whose every wise and witty word
Fell shy, half blushing to be heard.

Last, but ah! surely not least dear,
That blithe and buxom buccaneer,
Th' avenging goddess of her sex,
Born the base soul of man to vex,
And wring from him those tears and sighs
Tortured from woman's heart and eyes.
Ah! fury, fascinating, fair—
When shall I cease to think of her!

Paris, half Angel, half Grisette,
I would that I were with thee yet,
But London waits me, like a wife,—
London, the love of my whole life.

Tell her not, Paris, mercy me!
How I have flirted, dear, with thee.

ALFRED TENNYSON

(WESTMINSTER, OCTOBER 12, 1892)

Great man of song, whose glorious laurelled head
  Within the lap of death sleeps well at last,
Down the dark road, seeking the deathless dead,
  Thy faithful, fearless, shining soul hath passed.

Fame blows his silver trumpet o'er thy sleep,
  And Love stands broken by thy lonely lyre;
So pure the fire God gave this clay to keep,
  The clay must still seem holy for the fire.

Poor dupes of sense, we deem the close-shut eye,
  So faithful servant of his golden tongue,

Still holds the hoarded lights of earth and sky,
　　We deem the mouth still full of sleeping song.

We mourn as though the great good song he gave
　　Passed with the singer's own informing breath:
Ah, golden book, for thee there is no grave,
　　Thine is a rhyme that shall not taste of death.

Great wife of his great heart—'tis yours to mourn,
　　Son well-beloved, 'tis yours, who loved him so:
But we!—hath death one perfect page out-torn
　　From the great song whereby alone we know

The splendid spirit imperiously shy,—
　　Husband to you and father—we afar
Hail poet of God, and name as one should cry:
　　'Yonder a king, and yonder lo! a star!'

So great his song we deem a little while
　　That Song itself with his great voice hath fled,
So grand the toga-sweep of his great style,
　　So vast the theme on which his song was fed.

One sings a flower, and one a face, and one
　　Screens from the world a corner choice and small,
Each toy its little laureate hath, but none
　　Sings of the whole: yea, only he sang all.

Poor little bards, so shameless in your care
　　To snatch the mighty laurel from his head,
Have you no fear, dwarfs in the giant's chair,
　　How men shall laugh, remembering the dead?

Great is advertisement! 'tis almost fate,
　　But, little mushroom-men, of puff-ball fame,
Ah, do you dream to be mistaken great
　　And to be really great are just the same?

Ah, fools! he was a laureate ere one leaf
　　Of the great crown had whispered on his brows;
Fame shrilled his song, Love carolled it, and Grief
　　Blessed it with tears within her lonely house.

Fame loved him well, because he loved not Fame,
　　But Peace and Love, all other things before,
A man was he ere yet he was a name,
　　His song was much because his love was more.

PROFESSOR MINTO

Nature, that makes Professors all day long,
And, filling idle souls with idle song,
Turns out small Poets every other minute,
Made earth for men—but seldom puts men in it.

Ah, Minto, thou of that minority
Wert man of men—we had deep need of thee!
Had Heaven a deeper? Did the heavenly Chair
Of Earthly Love wait empty for thee there?

March 1, 1893.

ON MR. GLADSTONE'S RETIREMENT

The world grows Lilliput, the great men go;
  If greatness be, it wears no outer sign;
  No more the signet of the mighty line
Stamps the great brow for all the world to know.
Shrunken the mould of manhood is, and lo!
  Fragments and fractions of the old divine,
  Men pert of brain, planned on a mean design,
Dapper and undistinguished—such we grow.

No more the leonine heroic head,
  The ruling arm, great heart, and kingly eye;
No more th' alchemic tongue that turned poor themes
  Of statecraft into golden-glowing dreams;
  No more a man for man to deify:
Laurel no more—the heroic age is dead.

OMAR KHAYYÁM

(TO THE OMAR KHAYYÁM CLUB)

Great Omar, here to-night we drain a bowl
Unto thy long-since transmigrated soul,
  Ours all unworthy in thy place to sit,
Ours still to read in life's enchanted scroll.

For us like thee a little hour to stay,
For us like thee a little hour of play,
  A little hour for wine and love and song,
And we too turn the glass and take our way.

So many years your tomb the roses strew,
Yet not one penny wiser we than you,

The doubts that wearied you are with us still,
And, Heaven be thanked! your wine is with us too.

For, have the years a better message brought
To match the simple wisdom that you taught:
  Love, wine and verse, and just a little bread—
For these to live and count the rest as nought?

Therefore, Great Omar, here our homage deep
We drain to thee, though all too fast asleep
  In Death's intoxication art thou sunk
To know the solemn revels that we keep.

Oh, had we, best-loved Poet, but the power
From our own lives to pluck one golden hour,
And give it unto thee in thy great need,
How would we welcome thee to this bright bower!

O life that is so warm, 'twas Omar's too;
O wine that is so red, he drank of you:
  Yet life and wine must all be put away,
And we go sleep with Omar—yea, 'tis true.

And when in some great city yet to be
The sacred wine is spilt for you and me,
  To those great fames that we have yet to build,
We'll know as little of it all as he.

THE SECOND CRUCIFIXION

Loud mockers in the roaring street
  Say Christ is crucified again:
Twice pierced His gospel-bringing feet,
  Twice broken His great heart in vain.

I hear, and to myself I smile,
For Christ talks with me all the while.

No angel now to roll the stone
  From off His unawaking sleep,
In vain shall Mary watch alone,
  In vain the soldiers vigil keep.

Yet while they deem my Lord is dead
My eyes are on His shining head.

Ah! never more shall Mary hear
  That voice exceeding sweet and low
Within the garden calling clear:

Her Lord is gone, and she must go.

Yet all the while my Lord I meet
In every London lane and street.

Poor Lazarus shall wait in vain,
  And Bartimaeus still go blind;
The healing hem shall ne'er again
  Be touched by suffering humankind.

Yet all the while I see them rest,
The poor and outcast, in His breast.

No more unto the stubborn heart
  With gentle knocking shall He plead,
No more the mystic pity start,
  For Christ twice dead is dead indeed.

So in the street I hear men say,
Yet Christ is with me all the day.

AN IMPRESSION

The floating call of the cuckoo,
Soft little globes of bosom-shaped sound,
Came and went at the window;
And, out in the great green world,
Those maidens each morn the flowers
Opened their white little bodices wide to the sun:
And the man sighed—sighed—in his sleep,
And the woman smiled.

Then a lark staggered singing by
Up his shining ladder of dew,
And the airs of dawn walked softly about the room,
Filling the morning sky with the scent of the woman's hair,
And giving, in sweet exchange, its hawthorn and daisy breath:
And the man awoke with a sob—
But the woman dreamed.

NATURAL RELIGION

Up through the mystic deeps of sunny air
I cried to God—'O Father, art Thou there?'
Sudden the answer, like a flute, I heard:
It was an angel, though it seemed a bird.

FAITH REBORN

'The old gods pass,' the cry goes round;
'Lo! how their temples strew the ground';
Nor mark we where, on new-fledged wings,
Faith, like the phoenix, soars and sings.

HESPERIDES

Men say—beyond the western seas
  The happy isles no longer glow,
No sailor sights Hesperides,
  All that was long ago.

No longer in a glittering morn
  Their misty meadows flicker nigh,
No singing with the spray is borne,
  All that is long gone by.

To-day upon the golden beach
  No gold-haired guardian maidens stand,
No apples ripen out of reach,
  And none are mad to land.

The merchant-men, 'tis they say so,
  That trade across the western seas,
In hurried transit to and fro,
  About Hesperides.

But, Reader, not as these thou art,
  So, loose thy shallop from its hold,
And, trusting to the ancient chart,
  Thou 'lt make them as of old.

JENNY DEAD

Like a flower in the frost
  Sweet Jenny lies,
With her frail hands calmly crossed,
  And close-shut eyes.

Bring a candle, for the room
  Is dark and cold,
Antechamber of the tomb—
  O grief untold!

Like a snowdrift is her bed,
  Dinted the snow,
Faint frozen lines from foot to head,—
  She lies below.

Turn from off her shrouded face
  The frigid sheet....
Death hath doubled all her grace—
  O Jenny, sweet!

MY BOOKS

What are my books?—My friends, my loves,
  My church, my tavern, and my only wealth;
My garden: yea, my flowers, my bees, my doves;
  My only doctors—and my only health.

MAMMON

(FOR MR, G. F. WATTS'S PICTURE)

Mammon is this, of murder and of gold,
To-day, to-morrow, and ever from of old,
Th' Almighty God, and King of every land.
Man 'neath his foot, and woman 'neath his hand,
Kneel prostrate: he, 'tis meant to symbolise,
Steals our strong men and our sweet women buys.

O! rather grind me down into the dust
Than choose me for the vessel of thy lust.

ART

Art is a gipsy,
  Fickle as fair,
Good to kiss and flirt with,
  But marry—if you dare!

TO A POET

(TO EDMUND GOSSE)

Still towards the steep Parnassian way
The moon-led pilgrims wend,
Ah, who of all that start to-day
Shall ever reach the end?

Year after year a dream-fed band
That scorn the vales below,
And scorn the fatness of the land
To win those heights of snow,—

Leave barns and kine and flocks behind,
And count their fortune fair,
If they a dozen leaves may bind
Of laurel in their hair.

Like us, dear Poet, once you trod
That sweet moon-smitten way,
With mouth of silver sought the god
All night and all the day;

Sought singing, till in rosy fire
The white Apollo came,
And touched your brow, and wreathed your lyre,
And named you by his name;

And led you, loving, by the hand
To those grave laurelled bowers,
Where keep your high immortal band
Your high immortal hours.

Strait was the way, thorn-set and long—
Ah, tell us, shining there,
Is fame as wonderful as song?
And laurels in your hair!

A NEW YEAR LETTER

To Two Friends married in the New Year

(TO. MR. AND MRS. WELCH)

Another year to its last day,
Like a lost sovereign, runaway,
Tips down the gloomy grid of time:
In vain to holloa, 'Stop it! hey!'—
A cab-horse that has taken fright,
Be you a policeman, stop you may;
But not a sovereign mad with glee
That scampers to the grid, perdie,

And not a year that's taken flight;
To both 'tis just a grim good night.

But no! the imagery, say you,
Is wondrous witty—but not true;
For the old year that last night went
Has not been so much lost as spent:
You gave it in exchange to Death
For just twelve months of happy breath.

It was a ticket to admit
Two happy people close to sit—
A 'Season' ticket, one might say,
At Time's eternal passion play.

O magic overture of Spring,
O Summer like an Eastern King,
O Autumn, splendid widowed Queen,
O Winter, alabaster tomb
Where lie the regal twain serene,
Gone to their yearly doom.

But all you bought with that spent year,—
Ah, friends! it was as nothing, was it?
Nothing at all to hold compare
With what you buy with this New Year.
A home! ah me, you could not buy
Another half so precious toy,
With all the other years to come
As that grown-up doll's house—a home.

O wine upon its threshold stone,
And horse-shoes on the lintel of it,
And happy hearts to keep it warm,
And God Himself to love it!
Dear little nest built snug on bough
Within the World-Tree's mighty arms,
I would I knew a spell that charms
Eternal safety from the storm;

To give you always stars above,
And always roses on the bough—
But then the Tree's own root is Love,
Love, love, all love, I vow.

New Year 1893.

SNATCH

From tavern to tavern
  Youth passes along,
With an armful of girl
  And a heart full of song.

From flower to flower
  The butterfly sips,
O passionate limbs
  And importunate lips!

From candle to candle
  The moth loves to fly,
O sweet, sweet to burn!
  And still sweeter to die!

MY MAIDEN VOTE

(TO JOHN FRASER)

There, in my mind's-eye, pure it lay,
My lodger's vote! 'Twas mine to-day.
It seemed a sort of maidenhood,
My little power for public good,—
Oh keep it uncorrupted, pray!
And, when it must be given away,
See it be given with a sense
Of most uncanvassed innocence.
Alas!—but few there be that know't—
How grave a thing it is to vote!
For most men's votes are given, I hear,
Either for rhetoric or—beer.

A young man's vote—O fair estate!
Of the great tree electorate
A living leaf, of this great sea
A motive wave of empire I,
On this stupendous wheel—a fly.
O maiden vote, how pure must be
The party that is worthy thee!
And thereupon my mind began
That perfect government to plan,
The high millennium of man.

Then in my dream I saw arise
An England, ah! so fair and wise,
An England generously great,
No selfish island, but a state
Upon the world's bright forehead worn,
A mighty star of mighty morn.

And statesmen in that dream became
No tricksters of the petty aim,
Mere speculators in the rise
Of programmes and of party cries,
Expert in all those turns and tricks
That make this senate-house of ours,
Westminster, with its lordly towers,
The stock-exchange of politics.
But that ideal Parliament
Did all it said, said all it meant,
And every Minister of State
Was guileless—as a candidate.

Statesmen no more the tinker's way
Mended and patched from day to day,
Content with piecing part with part,
But took the mighty problem whole,
Beginning with the human heart:
For noble rulers make in vain
Unselfish laws for selfish men,
And give the whole wide world its vote,
But who is going to give it soul?

And then I dreamed had come to reign
True peace within our land again;
Not peace that rots the soul with ease,
Or those ignoble 'rivalries
Of peace' more murderous than war,
But just the simple peasant peace
The weary world is waiting for.
With simple food and simple wear
Go lots of love and little care,
And joy is saved from over-sweet
By struggle not too hard to bear.

So dreamed I on from dream to dream,
Till, slow returning to my theme,
Upon my vote I looked again—
To whom was I to give it then?
That uncorrupted maidenhood,
My little power for public good.
What party was there that I knew
That I might dare intrust it to,
A perfect party fair and square—
My House of Commons in the air?

Though called by many different names,
Each one professed the noblest aims;
Should all be right, 'twas logical
That I should give my vote to all!

And then, of parties old and new
Which one, if only one, were true?

The divination passed my skill,—
My maiden vote is maiden still.

THE ANIMALCULE ON MAN

An animalcule in my blood
  Rose up against me as I dreamed,
He was so tiny as he stood,
  You had not heard him, though he screamed.

He cried 'There is no Man!'
  And thumped the table with his fist,
Then died—his day was scarce a span,—
  That microscopic atheist.

Yet all the while his little soul
  Within what he denied did live,—
Poor part, how could he know the whole?
  And yet he was so positive!

And all the while he thus blasphemed
  My (solar) system went its round,
My heart beat on, my head still dreamed,—
  But my poor atheist was drowned.

COME, MY CELIA

Come, my Celia, let us prove,
While we may, how wise is love—
Love grown old and grey with years,
Love whose blood is thinned with tears.

Philosophic lover I,
Broke my heart, its love run dry,
And I warble passion's words
But to hear them sing like birds.

When the lightning struck my side,
Love shrieked and for ever died,
Leaving nought of him behind
But these playthings of the mind.

Now the real play is over

I can only act a lover,
Now the mimic play begins
With its puppet joys and sins.

When the heart no longer feels,
And the blood with caution steals,
Then, ah! then—my heart, forgive!—
Then we dare begin to live.

Dipped in Stygian waves of pain,
We can never feel again;
Time may hurl his deadliest darts,
Love may practise all his arts;

Like some Balder, lo! we stand
Safe 'mid hurtling spear and brand,
Only Death—ah! sweet Death, throw!—
Holds the fatal mistletoe.

Let the young unconquered soul
Love the unit as the whole,
Let the young uncheated eye
Love the face fore-doomed to die:

But, my Celia, not for us
Pleasures half so hazardous;
Let us set our hearts on play,
'Tis, alas! the only way—

Make of life the jest it is,
Laugh and fool and (maybe!) kiss,
Never for a moment, dear,
Love so well to risk a fear.

Is not this, my Celia, say,
The only wise—and weary—way?

TIME'S MONOTONE

  Autumn and Winter,
  Summer and Spring—
Hath Time no other song to sing?
Weary we grow of the changeless tune—
  June—December,
  December—June!

Time, like a bird, hath but one song,
  One way to build, like a bird hath he;
Thus hath he built so long, so long,

Thus hath he sung—Ah me!

Time, like a spider, knows, be sure,
  One only wile, though he seems so wise:
Death is his web, and Love his lure,
  And you and I his flies.

   'Love!' he sings
  In the morning clear,
   'Love! Love! Love!'
  And you never hear
  How, under his breath,
  He whispers, 'Death!
  Death! Death!'

Yet Time—'tis the strangest thing of all—
  Knoweth not the sense of the words he saith;
Eternity taught him his parrot-call
  Of 'Love and Death.'

Year after year doth the old man climb
  The mountainous knees of Eternity,
But Eternity telleth nothing to Time—
  It may not be.

COR CORDIUM

O GOLDEN DAY! O SILVER NIGHT!

O golden day! O silver night!
  That brought my own true love at last,
Ah, wilt thou drop from out our sight,
  And drown within the past?

One wave, no more, in life's wide sea,
  One little nameless crest of foam,
The day that gave her all to me
  And brought us to our home.

Nay, rather as the morning grows
  In flush, and gleam, and kingly ray,
While up the heaven the sun-god goes,
  So shall ascend our day.

And when at last the long night nears,
  And love grows angel in the gloom,
Nay, sweetheart, what of fears and tears?—
  The stars shall see us home.

LOVE'S EXCHANGE

Simple am I, I care no whit
  For pelf or place,
It is enough for me to sit
  And watch Dulcinea's face;
To mark the lights and shadows flit
  Across the silver moon of it.

I have no other merchandise,
  No stocks or shares,
No other gold but just what lies
  In those deep eyes of hers;
And, sure, if all the world were wise,
It too would bank within her eyes.

I buy up all her smiles all day
  With all my love,
And sell them back, cost-price, or, say,
  A kiss or two above;
It is a speculation fine,
The profit must be always mine.

The world has many things, 'tis true,
  To fill its time,
Far more important things to do
  Than making love and rhyme;
Yet, if it asked me to advise,
I'd say—buy up Dulcinea's eyes!

TO A SIMPLE HOUSEWIFE

Who dough shall knead as for God's sake
  Shall fill it with celestial leaven,
And every loaf that she shall bake
  Be eaten of the Blest in heaven.

LOVE'S WISDOM

Sometimes my idle heart would roam
  Far from its quiet happy nest,
To seek some other newer home,
  Some unaccustomed Best:
But ere it spreads its foolish wings,

'Heart, stay at home, be wise!' Love's wisdom sings.

Sometimes my idle heart would sail
  From out its quiet sheltered bay,
To tempt a less pacific gale,
  And oceans far away:
But ere it shakes its foolish wings,
'Heart, stay at home, be wise!' Love's wisdom sings.

Sometimes my idle heart would fly,
  Mothlike, to reach some shining sin,
It seems so sweet to burn and die
  That wondrous light within:
But ere it burns its foolish wings,
'Heart, stay at home, be wise!' Love's wisdom sings.

HOME ...

'We're going home!' I heard two lovers say,
  They kissed their friends and bade them bright good-byes;
  I hid the deadly hunger in my eyes,
And, lest I might have killed them, turned away.
Ah, love! we too once gambolled home as they,
  Home from the town with such fair merchandise,—
  Wine and great grapes—the happy lover buys:
A little cosy feast to crown the day.

Yes! we had once a heaven we called a home
  Its empty rooms still haunt me like thine eyes,
When the last sunset softly faded there;
Each day I tread each empty haunted room,
  And now and then a little baby cries,
  Or laughs a lovely laughter worse to bear.

LOVE'S LANDMARKS

The woods we used to walk, my love,
  Are woods no more,
But' villas' now with sounding names—
  All name and door.

The pond, where, early on in March,
  The yellow cup
Of water-lilies made us glad,
  Is now filled up.

But ah! what if they fill or fell
  Each pond, each tree,
What matters it to-day, my love,

To me—to thee?

The jerry-builder may consume,
  A greedy moth,
God's mantle of the living green,
  I feel no wrath;

Eat up the beauty of the world,
  And gorge his fill
On mead and winding country lane,
  And grassy hill.

I only laugh, for now of these
  I have no care,
Now that to me the fair is foul,
  And foul as fair.

IF, AFTER ALL …!

This life I squander, hating the long days
That will not bring me either Rest or Thee,
This health I hack and ravage as with knives,
These nerves I fain would shatter, and this heart
I fain would break—this heart that, traitor-like,
Beats on with foolish and elastic beat:
If, after all, this life I waste and kill
Should still be thine, may still be lived for thee!
And this the dreadful trial of my love,
This silence and this blank that makes me mad,
That I be man to-day of all the days
My one poor hope of meeting thee again—
If Death be Love, and God's great purpose kind!

Oh, love, if some day on the heavenly stair
A wild ecstatic moment we should stand,
And I, all hungry for your eyes and hair,
Should meet instead your great accusing gaze,
And hear, instead of welcome into heaven:
'Ah! hadst thou but been true! but manfully
Borne the high pangs that all high souls must bear,
Nor fled to low nepenthes for your pain!
Hadst said—"Is she not here? more reason then
To live as though still guarded by her eyes,
Cleaner my thought, and purer be my deed;
True will I be, though God Himself be false!"'

Oh, hadst thou thus been man, to-day had we
Walked on together undivided now—
But now a thousand flaming years must pass,
And all the trial be gone o'er again.

She loved the Autumn, I the Spring,
Sad all the songs she loved to sing;
And in her face was strangely set
Some great inherited regret.

Some look in all things made her sigh,
Yea! sad to her the morning sky:
'So sad! so sad its beauty seems'—
I hear her say it still in dreams.

But when the day grew grey and old,
And rising stars shone strange and cold,
Then only in her face I saw
A mystic glee, a joyous awe.

Spirit of Sadness, in the spheres
Is there an end of mortal tears?
Or is there still in those great eyes
That look of lonely hills and skies?

AN INSCRIPTION

Precious the box that Mary brake
Of spikenard for her Master's sake,
But ah! it held nought half so dear
As the sweet dust that whitens here.
The greater wonder who shall say:
To make so white a soul of clay,
From clay to win a face so fair,
Those strange great eyes, that sunlit hair
A-ripple o'er her witty brain,—
Or turn all back to dust again.

Who knows—but, in some happy hour,
The God whose strange alchemic power
Wrought her of dust, again may turn
To woman this immortal urn.

SONG

She's somewhere in the sunlight strong,
  Her tears are in the falling rain,
She calls me in the wind's soft song,
  And with the flowers she comes again.

Yon bird is but her messenger,
  The moon is but her silver car;
Yea! sun and moon are sent by her,
  And every wistful waiting star.

Richard Le Gallienne – A Concise Bibliography

My Ladies' Sonnets and Other Vain and Amatorious Verses (1887)
Volumes in Folio (1889) poems
George Meredith: Some Characteristics (1890)
The Book-Bills of Narcissus (1891)
English Poems (1892)
The Religion of a Literary Man (1893)
Robert Louis Stevenson: An Elegy and Other Poems (1895)
Quest of the Golden Girl (1896) novel
Prose Fancies (1896)
Retrospective Reviews (1896)
Rubaiyat of Omar Khayyam (1897)
If I Were God (1897)
The Romance of Zion Chapel (1898)
In Praise of Bishop Valentine (1898)
Young Lives (1899)
Sleeping Beauty and Other Prose Fancies (1900)
The Worshipper of The Image (1900)
The Love Letters of the King, or The Life Romantic (1901)
An Old Country House (1902)
Odes from the Divan of Hafiz (1903) translation
Old Love Stories Retold (1904)
Painted Shadows (1904)
Romances of Old France (1905)
Little Dinners with the Sphinx and other Prose Fancies (1907)
Omar Repentant (1908)
Wagner's Tristan and Isolde (1909) Translator
Attitudes and Avowals (1910) essays
October Vagabonds (1910)
New Poems (1910)
The Maker of Rainbows and Other Fairy-Tales and Fables (1912)
The Lonely Dancer and Other Poems (1913)
The Highway to Happiness (1913)
Vanishing Roads and Other Essays (1915)
The Silk-Hat Soldier and Other Poems in War Time (1915)
The Chain Invisible (1916)
Pieces of Eight (1918)
The Junk-Man and Other Poems (1920)
A Jongleur Strayed (1922) poems
Woodstock: An Essay (1923)
The Romantic '90s (1925) memoirs
The Romance of Perfume (1928)
There Was a Ship (1930)

From a Paris Garret (1936) memoirs
The Diary of Samuel Pepys (editor)